PRAYING THE CHARTRES LABYRINTH
A PILGRIM'S GUIDEBOOK

Jill Kimberly Hartwell Geoffrion

THE PILGRIM PRESS

CLEVELAND

The Pilgrim Press, 700 Prospect Avenue, Cleveland, Ohio 44115-1100
thepilgrimpress.com
© 2006 Jill Kimberly Hartwell Geoffrion

Image of the Chartres Cathedral © 2003 Robert Ferré, used by permission. ■ All photos
© Jill Kimberly Hartwell Geoffrion, except the following, used by permission: ■ © Cheryl Felicia
Dudley: Spiritual Practices; Identity Shifts; The Chartres Cathedral; Unity and Diversity; Beauty;
Distractions; How Long?; Local Devotional Practices; Stained Glass Windows; Sharing Gratitude;
Thank-you Letter ■ © Timothy Charles Geoffrion: Surprises; Leave Taking; Walking into the
Truth; Forgetting and Remembering; The Gift of Each Moment; Where to Go; Why Am I Here?
■ © Timothy Clarence Geoffrion: Staying Present ■ © Daniel Eugene Geoffrion: Deciding to Go

Scripture quotations are from the New Revised Standard Version of the Bible, © 1989 by the
Division of Christian Education of the National Council of Churches of Christ in the United States
of America and are used by permission. Changes have been made for inclusivity.

10   09   08   07   06   5   4   3   2   1

Library of Congress Cataloging-in-Publication Data

Geoffrion, Jill Kimberly Hartwell, 1958–
    Praying the Chartres labyrinth : a pilgrim's guidebook / Jill Kimberly Hartwell Geoffrion.
    p.   cm.
    Includes bibliographical references.
    ISBN 0-8298-1715-8 (pbk.)
    1. Labyrinths—Religious aspects—Christianity.   2. Prayer—Christianity.   3. Spiritual life—
Christianity.   4. Christian pilgrims and pilgrimages.   5. Cathadrale de Chartres.   I. Title.
    BV4509.5.G448   2005
    263'.042445124—dc22
                                                            2005054922

ISBN 13 : 978-0-8298-1715-7
ISBN 10 : 0-8298-1715-8

Printed in China

Contents

Contents

Contents

Contents

F O R E W O R D

O ver the past thirty-nine years I have been to Chartres Cathedral in France forty-nine times. For sixteen years I took groups on pilgrimage to France, two of which included Jill Geoffrion. In Jill I have found someone who loves the cathedral as dearly as I do. Through the years I have met many others who appreciate Chartres. Père François Legaux, the former rector, affectionately called it "my cathedral." Monsieur Dartus Yves chooses to spend his time in the shadow of the cathedral rather than chasing after the glittering illusions of society. John James studied the cathedral for six years, stone by stone, until the masons came alive through their styles, templates, and geometries. There are others, many others, but I can think of no one to whom the cathedral speaks more directly and more personally, and who responds in kind, than Jill Kimberly Hartwell Geoffrion.

Such a gift is rare. More common are the tourists descending from their huge buses for two hours in Chartres before rushing on to Versailles. For others, Chartres is a place for speculation and silly faux mysteries. Books on sacred sites often describe no more about Chartres than the presence of a Druid well, a black madonna, and seeming alignment with other sites. All they miss in such descriptions is the entire cathedral, what it is, how it came to be, what it represents, and what it offers to us now. The fact is, the truth is far more engaging than bizzarre theories suggesting Templars built the cathedral or that the Holy Grail is buried beneath the labyrinth.

To learn for yourself the truth about Chartres Cathedral, follow Jill's gentle instructions and guidance. The secret of Chartres Cathedral is exactly this: There is no secret! I am reminded of the opening line of Michael Schneider's book on sacred geometry: "The universe may be a mystery, but it's no secret." The cathedral is wide open and available to all who sincerely seek its inspiration and blessing. The value of Jill's book is that she gives a helpful variety of formats for getting to know and experience the real Chartres Cathedral.

Chartres Cathedral originated during a brief window in time in the twelfth century when a fortuitous combination of circumstances led to the development of the Gothic style: The weather improved, the political situation was stable, there was relative peace, the economy was expanding, and the population growing. The Virgin Mary was seen as an effective intercessor who could assure one's passage into heaven. The end result was a positive outlook coupled with soaring hope and devotion, which Will Durant has called the Age of Faith. It was this elevation of spirit that came to be expressed in towering, light-filled cathedrals of the Gothic style.

Gothic architecture took a hundred years of experimentation to evolve, mostly in the Paris Basin. It is as if each element—pointed arches, flying buttresses, triforiums, and more—was like the invention of a new instrument. Then, at Chartres, for the first time, the entire orchestra played—and what a beautiful song it was. The scale was unprecedented in height and width and the size of the clerestory windows. Notre Dame in Paris, started decades earlier, was subsequently rebuilt to incorporate some of the new advances. Chartres became the model for all Gothic churches. Others were built larger and more ornate, as the orchestra continued to play more complex variations on a theme, but it all started at Chartres, which made the others possible.

Because of its obscure location, Chartres remains the least changed and most authentic example of a Gothic church. The magnificent art was done not for the personal glory and recognition of the artist, as would happen a few centuries later in the Renaissance, but for the glory of God. Thus, neither the artists nor the masons of Chartres cathedral signed their work. (It is for this reason that as a labyrinth maker, I also never sign my work.)

During this window of time, all intellectual output—of the famous School of Chartres, of scholasticism and neoplatonism, of the seven liberal arts and sacred geometry, of the knowledge pouring into France from the Islamic world—was informed by a single purpose: How it addressed one's relationship with the divine. In that golden twelfth century, God was the measure of all things. Very soon after the cathedral was completed, the world changed. The Hundred Years War, the plague, the Renaissance, the age of science, the industrial revolution—all led to our modern, secular, scientific, commercial world. Now, towering over our cities are not magnificent cathedrals designed to be God's home on earth, but rather banks and office buildings. Man has become the measure of all things, with the standard being the size of the profit and the amount of political power.

The power of Chartres Cathedral is that it represents something older, something deeper, something more spiritual and mystical. Once I was in the cathedral as a family entered, including a boy of about seven years old. His head kept tilting back further and further as he strove to see the full height of the nave. He then let out a very audible and awe-filled, "Wow-w-w-w-w-w-w-w." That's what Chartres is all about. Somewhere in heaven the master mason of Chartres smiled and said, "He got it." So, too, does Jill. Jill Geoffrion gets it. She has learned to speak the language and do the practices necessary for an effective and meaningful pilgrimage to Chartres. She teaches us that language in this book.

Take Jill's book with you and go to Chartres, an hour southwest of Paris. Make it a real pilgrimage. Stay at least a week if you can, although a month would be better. You will find that Chartres Cathedral is huge, but it won't dwarf you. Rather, it will expand you. It is impressive, but not intimidating. It will inspire you. The physical building, while magnificent, is still only the container for our human experience. It is a place whose proportions and sounds and gem-like glowing windows are meant to transport us far beyond our ordinary lives into the realms of the infinite. Such, too, is the purpose of pilgrimage.

But there is a condition. We must be willing. We must ask. And we must listen to hear the answer. Jill's four stages of walking the labyrinth can equally be the stages of a pilgrimage: ask, listen, receive, and be grateful. It is this process that is so beautifully presented in this book. There is no one better suited or more qualified or more Chartres-filled to point the way than Jill Geoffrion. She could have kept her knowledge to herself, continuing to go to Chartres on her own to be filled and recharged. I can picture her, sitting alone to one side of the labyrinth, head bowed, heart open, her notebook at the ready. But instead, to our benefit, Jill has agreed to take us with her, showing us the way, step by step. This is a wonderful gift to all who read this book. Thank you, Jill. Thank you, thank you.

—*Robert Ferré*

DEDICATIONS AND ACKNOWLEDGMENTS

*It is a joy to dedicate this work
to two fellow pilgrims
who share a deep love for Chartres Cathedral:*

Cheryl Felicia Dudley,
my dear friend,
whose invitation to take a
mid-winter pilgrimage to Chartres
rekindled the fire that was needed
to move this book ahead,

and

Timothy Clarence Geoffrion,
my husband,
whose support
I experience at every turn.

Dedications and Acknowledgments

A special thanks to three "angels" whose support I felt each time I entered the cathedral to work on this book: **Monsieur Christian Gaudiniére**, former head of security, **Madame Patricia Devriendt**, welcomer for groups to the cathedral, and **Monsieur Dartus Yves**, "chanteur de la cathédral," who greets all at the doors.

I would also like to express my gratitude to **Robert Ferré,** who introduced me to the concept of using the labyrinth with sincerity in 1996 when we were on pilgrimage in Chartres.

Dedications and Acknowledgments

Thanks to
Linda Campbell,
Kate Christianson,
Cheryl Dudley,
Robert Ferré,
Dan Geoffrion,
Tim Geoffrion,
Lea Goode-Harris,
Lucy Hartwell,
Lyndall Johnson,
Kimberly Lowelle Saward,
and Kristine Thompson,
whose careful review of my manuscript
and helpful comments guided my reworking of this book.

I am indebted to my editor,
Ulrike Guthrie.
Her wise suggestions and commitment to this project
strengthened it immensely.

How to Use This Book

Chartres Cathedral is for me a place like no other. It serves as a physical symbol of the splendor, kindness, and majesty of God. The cathedral's architecture communicates in a language my body knows and loves; its beauty is deeply moving. The building's clarion call to faith inspires me. The sacred messages communicated through stone, glass, light, and darkness have been profoundly influential. Love and truth dwell within the walls of Chartres Cathedral; they have greeted me over and over in expected and surprising ways. Spending time in this magnificent church not only helps me to feel grounded, it opens my heart so that transformation in every area of my life becomes possible.

On the floor of Chartres Cathedral is a circular design whose diameter is forty-two feet, three and one-half inches. An interest in this labyrinth brought me back to the cathedral that I had studied as a collegiate art history student while living in Paris. Though often covered with chairs in modern times, it is still visible for it spans the entire width of the church's nave! When tourists enter the cathedral from the west, as most do, and walk toward the front of the church, they pass over the center of the labyrinth.

In recent times, many pilgrims have come to experience this ancient pathway of prayer that was installed as part of the floor around 1201 C.E. Some think of this labyrinth as a fractal of the whole cathedral. Others understand it to be a lovely symbol that holds profound invitations to sacred connections.

Friends sometimes inquire, "Do you love Chartres Cathedral?" and "Do you love the labyrinth?" "Yes!" I answer enthusiastically. Loving a building or a floor pattern may sound strange, but those who have spent time in the cathedral and have experienced its labyrinth are likely to smile knowingly. I love the cathedral and labyrinth because through them God's love profoundly engages me. It has been my deep joy and great privilege to travel as a pilgrim to Chartres Cathedral fourteen times. It is my home away from home. There is nowhere on the globe I feel more alive or more connected to the Deep Mystery of Reality. I long for others to experience God in this space.

Those planning a visit to Chartres often ask, "What should I do and see when I'm in the Chartres Cathedral?" Being only an hour outside of Paris, travelers to France often take the train or autoroute to visit this world-renowned monument. My advice starts with a simple instruction, "Walk all the way around the outside and inside of the church and notice where your heart beats faster, or where your body wants to pray. Once you've made the tour, go back to the place that drew you the most, and stay there as long as you can—at least fifteen minutes. If you can, be there for an hour or two. It will be a much more meaningful experience."

For those who want a longer, more complete answer, I've written this book. Its pages are filled with suggestions of how to glean the most meaning from your pilgrimage. There is much about Chartres Cathedral that I still have to learn. Yet this

I know: God can be experienced there. This book will help you explore and understand your experiences more fully.

Use this book in ways that support the purposes and flow of your pilgrimage. Think of it as a traveling companion who can point out relevant information, ask you questions, make suggestions, or remind you to stay on track. It is meant to inspire and support you as you journey toward spiritual maturity. At the bottom of each page is a question, the beginning of a sentence, or a suggestion. They are included so that you can explore your own pilgrimage experiences in the deepest ways possible. Use the blank space that is included to write, draw, or doodle; let your creativity flow freely! Be sure to revisit pages that speak to your needs the most directly. Use the margins for notes, suggestions that you might want to share with future pilgrims, and questions that you want to consider later.

If you cannot visit Chartres in person, you can still use the book as a companion on mini-pilgrimages to local labyrinths or other places of prayer. Most of the suggested labyrinth exercises can be easily adapted and used anywhere.

May you find the courage to make the pilgrimage that is in your heart and mind. May this book help you mine its riches.

Part One

PREPARATION FOR PILGRIMAGE

Why leave the familiar in search of distant destinations?

How does one move gracefully from routine to unpredictability?

When is the "right" time to go? These are some of the many

questions that would-be pilgrims ponder.

Each pilgrimage is unique; each pilgrim travels differently.

Yet there are some common themes and experiences that those

journeying for spiritual purposes encounter and embody.

In this section you are invited to explore the experiences and

meanings of the first phase of your pilgrimage, deciding to

go and getting ready.

O N E

Readying Yourself

The decision to make a pilgrimage usually develops over time.
When you begin to make plans, another phase of preparation has
begun. The value of readying yourself for pilgrimage is often
underestimated. The more you are willing to prepare, the more you
will be able to receive from the experience. This chapter encourages
you to prepare thoughtfully and prayerfully.

Why Make A Pilgrimage?

People answer in all sorts of ways:

It was time. I was curious. Expressing my gratitude to God motivated me. I needed healing. There was an unexplainable push. Why not? Things were shifting and I thought it would help me gain clarity. I had been dreaming about it for years. I was lonely for my spiritual home. I couldn't get the idea out of my head. I was longing for more time to spend with God and myself. I felt desperate. I thought it might help bring me some peace. It was as if a magnet were pulling me.

What is motivating me to consider going on pilgrimage?

Wait

If you can stay home, do.

Why begin a pilgrimage
if you don't feel compelled?

Spiritual desire is unpredictable
and unrelenting.

There is a time for everything;
it is worth waiting until you can resist no longer.

It is time to . . .

Deciding to Go

I want something to be different. I'm afraid of change.
I know I am ready. I won't be prepared.
This will work with my schedule. What won't get done while I'm away?
What regrets will haunt me if I don't say, "Yes"? Why commit myself?
I've made up my mind. This might be a huge mistake.
What if something happens? What if nothing happens?
My heart knows there is only one answer. My mind has so many questions.

As I'm deciding to go . . .

Getting Ready

Some say that a pilgrimage begins the moment one decides, "I'm going."

Most often there is a period of time between "I'm planning on it" and the actual departure date.

If your goal is to be intentional about preparing, what will help most?

The only way to answer that question wisely is to ask another, "Why is it important to make this pilgrimage at this time?"

I'm going on pilgrimage now because . . .

Helpful Preparations

I'm going;
I'm not gone yet.
Those preparing for pilgrimage straddle these two realities.

Prayer, reflection, labyrinth walking, talking with others, fasting, journaling,
collecting what will be needed, meditating, reading, stretching,
and other spiritual disciplines can prepare a pilgrim
for the departure as well as all that lies ahead.

I am preparing for my pilgrimage by . . .

Spiritual Practices

If one is not intentional,
many opportunities for spiritual growth may be missed
while on pilgrimage.

Ponder and answer the question:
Which spiritual practices
will help me mine the riches of the journey ahead?

Spiritual practices that can help me now . . .

My plan to incorporate them into my pilgrimage include . . .

Sharing the Spiritual Nature of the Trip

Sometimes when people hear about a pilgrimage,
they say things like "I hope it's a great trip" or "Have fun!"

Responding to others' lack of understanding
calls for patience, graciousness, and gentle clarity.

Communicating our sacred hopes to others can be challenging,
especially since we aren't sure of what lies ahead.

Consider how you can answer the question,
"Where you are going?"
to include some reflections on the unspoken query,
"Why you are going?"

When talking with others about my pilgrimage, I want to communicate . . .

Purpose

If pilgrimage is an external expression of an internal reality,
what is moving within?

It may be difficult to answer;
it may be even more of a challenge to keep wondering
without settling for a simple response.

Exploring the terrain of one's heart and mind
makes travel of distance and landscape seem easy.

Moving within me . . .

Packing Intentionally

"What will support my prayer?"
The pilgrim asks this question over and over, even when packing.
The answer depends on the purpose of this journey.
The needs when one is healing
are different than the needs of one who is setting off
to learn more about letting go.

As each item enters your luggage, ask it, "How will you help me?"

Take carefully chosen clothes, shoes, toiletries, art supplies,
books, a Bible, a journal, and other items
that will help make your pilgrimage what it needs to be.

Leave the rest home.

For me to pack wisely will mean . . .

Never Quite Ready

Is there a pilgrim anywhere
who wouldn't admit,
"I'm less prepared
than I would like"?

Without censoring yourself,
write several sentences that each begin,

"If I were more prepared . . ."

Surprises

I can't know what is ahead.
Unpredictability can be exhilarating
as well as frightening.
Yet, one thing is certain,
God's grace will surprise me.

I am preparing myself for the
surprises I'll experience by . . .

Part Two

SEPARATION FROM HOME

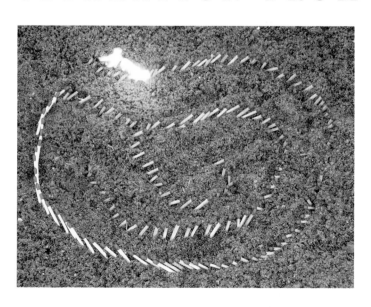

Preparation leads to that moment when a threshold must be crossed. When it is time, one leaves home for the pilgrimage destination. This chapter supports the pilgrim during this time of transition.

TWO

Leave Taking

Transition times are often filled with both excitement and dread. By staying present to all the emotions that are being experienced, the pilgrim can begin to enter fully into the shifting reality that occurs when leaving home. Use the suggestions in this chapter to pay attention to the gifts of this important period of change.

Walking into the Truth

Medieval pilgrims faced many physical dangers.
They left home with no certainty that they would return.
They stepped into an unsure future.

Modern pilgrims face less physical danger,
but by putting themselves in new situations and environments
they too step into a future that is unknown.

Although I am uncertain of what is ahead . . .

Letting Go

Every pilgrim has good-byes to say.
Every pilgrim must entrust to God
those things that cannot be attended to from a distance.

God, I commend to your care . . .

Thy Will Be Done

Leaving the familiar
involves relinquishing routine and security.

It also invites new routines
that can offer temporary sanctuary.

Acknowledge in prayer
the truth you are embodying as you leave.

Let "Thy will be done" travel with you as you repeat it throughout each day.

Going Away, Going Toward

Pilgrims are moving away from
focusing externally.
They are heading toward
internal realms.

They move away from activity
while heading toward greater stillness.

They move away from schedules
dictated by others' needs
while heading toward doing things
when the time seems right.

They move away from rootedness
while heading toward their deepest root.

I am moving away from . . .

I am heading toward . . .

Forgetting and Remembering

"What did I forget?"
is a question that plagues many travelers, including pilgrims.

After setting off, it is also important to ask,
"What do I need to forget?"
and "What do I need to remember?"

I need to forget...

I need to remember...

Identity Shifts

Upon leaving one's family, friends, and community,
a pilgrim is suddenly alone
in a way that probably feels very unfamiliar.
You can now explore your identity from fresh angles.

*Using the space below draw a picture of yourself
as you imagine yourself when returning from
this pilgrimage. (A word picture will also do.)*

The Gift of Each Moment

Fear
is a familiar traveling partner
for many pilgrims.

It whispers messages like
"No one will ever understand what has happened."
Or
"Others will judge my experiences of God."

Pilgrims are wise to respond firmly,
"If I am present to my experience now,
I will discover how to express my experiences to others."

Speaking to one's fears helps diminish their power.
Say out loud five times,
or write in your journal five times,
"If I am present to my experience now,
I will discover how to express my experiences to others."

Part Three

EXPERIENCING THE PILGRIMAGE DESTINATION

For some, arriving at a pilgrimage site and offering a prayer of gratitude is enough. The goal has been reached. For many others, meaning comes when the pilgrim lingers at the destination long enough to explore its riches, pray for extended periods of time, and reflect deeply.

The following chapters invite the pilgrim to explore the outer landscape of Chartres Cathedral and the inner landscape of faith that it is designed to inspire and nurture. The labyrinth is introduced within the cathedral context that has housed it for the last eight hundred years.

T H R E E

Arriving

Whether seen while on foot across a cornfield, through the windshield of a car on the highway, or from the window as a train approaches the town, the first glimpse of Chartres Cathedral causes great joy. The goal of the pilgrimage is in sight! The selections in this chapter are designed to welcome you to Chartres and to invite you to begin to familiarize yourself with this amazing church.

Questions Worth Considering

How many different ways can you answer the question "Why have I come?"

What fears would you like to release now that you are arriving at a place that supports change?

What stories have you been telling yourself about this pilgrimage?

What emotions have you not felt on your journey thus far?

How are your expectations changing?

What does it feel like to be in Chartres?

My questions . . .

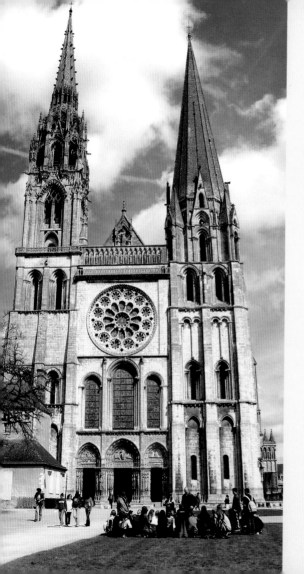

Wow!

What sort of vision
inspired a building
that first takes one's breath away,
only to give it back?

*My first impressions
of Chartres Cathedral . . .*

Tourists and Pilgrims

Tourists come to see what there is to see.
Pilgrims come to make sacred connections.

Tourists sometimes act like pilgrims.
Pilgrims sometimes act like tourists.

Identity matters less than intention.

My pilgrim and tourist intentions . . .

Circumambulating

How do you ready yourself to enter
the "destination" of your pilgrimage?

There is a moment of arrival,
but there is also
a process of arriving.

Many religious traditions
encourage the practice
of circling a holy site
before entering it.

Orient yourself
by slowly walking around
the outside of the cathedral.

Even though part of me
wanted to rush right in . . .

Walking Around—Literally

Over the centuries, many have found it helpful
to walk around the perimeter of a sacred site
before entering it.

Both external and internal preparations are useful.

Use the time that you circumambulate the church
to prepare yourself
for the next phase of your pilgrimage,
the entering of the cathedral.

Look, pray, listen, feel, notice, open.

As I prepare to enter the cathedral . . .

The Architecture of Truth

Architect John James speaks of Chartres Cathedral
as embodying an architecture of truth.

After studying the cathedral literally stone by stone,
James has concluded that those who built it
were trying to show the truth of the building
in the building itself.

Look at the cathedral again.
Gaze at truth.

As I look at truth, I . . .

Listen To Your Longings

When getting to know
this pilgrimage site,
listen to the voice
of your longings.

Your heart can lead you
to places you are
hoping to discover.

*Words and images
related to my longings . . .*

Medieval Sensibilities

There have been relatively few structural changes to Chartres Cathedral
since it was dedicated in 1260 C.E.
The St. Piat and Vendôme chapels, the clock, as well as the North Tower
are the noticeable exceptions.

The building you see and experience
is strikingly similar to what ancient pilgrims knew.

Through attention
and intention,
you can receive the gifts of the past,
and apply them to the needs of the present.

Ancient and modern realities are leading me toward . . .

The Invitation to Enter

The inside of the cathedral will make more sense
now that you have taken time to ready yourself.

Throughout the ages pilgrims have entered the cathedral
through the west doors.

Take a moment to appreciate how the building is inviting you in,
even if your way seems blocked
due to external or internal causes.

As I ready myself to enter the cathedral . . .

F O U R

The Chartres Cathedral

A majestic building with its world-renowned collection of medieval stained glass windows and sculptures, this functioning church is located just an hour outside of Paris, France. It welcomes tens of thousands of tourists and pilgrims each year.

Walking into Chartres Cathedral is an unforgettable experience. While the eyes adjust to the subdued light, the spirit is likely to soar in awe! This chapter is designed to orient pilgrims who have come here to pray.

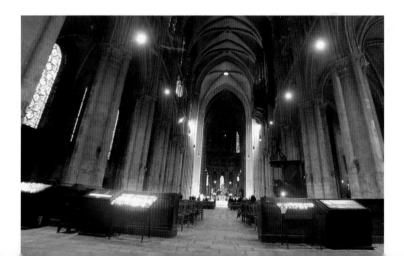

Life-size Magnificence

As one steps inside the west door
of this amazing cathedral,
beauty presents itself first
to the body, then to the mind.

How can one feel so at home
in a space this grand?
As the body relaxes, the mind reels.

While the eyes adjust, light begs
to be understood in new ways.
But first one must decide what to do
with the urge to laugh with joy!

*My initial experience of the inside
of Chartres Cathedral . . .*

Life

Chartres is a cathedral of life.

No one is buried within its walls.

It is a church dedicated to Mary, the bearer of Life.

It is an earthly reminder of the New Jerusalem,
a biblical symbol of eternal life.

One can almost hear an echo from the Gospel of John
reverberating off the walls:
"What has come into being in the Word was life,
and the life was the light of all people." (1:3–4)

Write a poem or song about
Chartres Cathedral starting with
Life . . .

Dedication to Mary

Chartres Cathedral was built in honor of Mary,
the mother of Jesus.

Statues and stained glass portraits
remind pilgrims at every turn of Mary's graciousness
and power.

The cathedral relic,
an ancient piece of cloth Mary is said to have worn
either during the annunciation or at Jesus' birth,
has drawn pilgrims to Chartres for centuries.

My encounters with Mary in the cathedral . . .

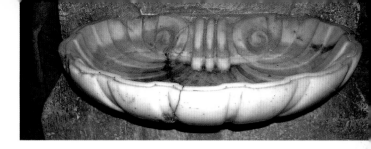

Getting Oriented

Upon entering the cathedral,
modern-day pilgrims orient themselves by making the sign of the cross
with holy water.

Ancient pilgrims oriented themselves through understanding of the theology
behind the architecture of the church.

North in a medieval cathedral
represented the Old Testament times and truths.

South corresponded to the New Testament and its messages.

East, where the altar was located,
directed one's attention to resurrection and heaven.

West, where the pilgrim would enter,
held reminders of death, judgment, and the end of time.

To orient myself in the church . . .

The Blessing of Lingering Prayers

Chartres Cathedral
and the earlier sanctuaries built here
have been receptacles of billions of prayers.

As you enter the church,
be aware that the gentle vibration of heart-felt prayer
will greet and envelop you.

Know that the prayers you offer in this sacred site
will reverberate long after you have gone.

*My experiences of the ambience of prayer in
Chartres Cathedral . . .*

Unity and Diversity

There is a sense of unity
that is palpable inside Chartres Cathedral.

Students of the cathedral
are quick to point out the many internal
architectural discrepancies.

Yet the cathedral communicates
a unified message of beauty.
The architectural diversity that exists
does not disrupt. It adds interest.

Sketch relating to my perceptions
of unity and diversity
as embodied by the cathedral:

45

Proportions of Growth

Living things grow in a proportional way.
Plants do. Humans too.
The same ratio of growth that is manifest in our bodies
is found throughout Chartres Cathedral.
Our bodies resonate with the message of growth,
even when it is communicated with stone and space.

Images and words relating to growth
inspired by my experiences in Chartres Cathedral . . .

Heaven on Earth

Modern pilgrims to Chartres Cathedral
are often unaware
that they are standing inside
an earthly representation of heaven.

This church was designed
to prefigure the heavenly Jerusalem
spoken of in the biblical book of Revelation.

One need not understand this to experience it.

Glimpses, echoes, or visions of heaven I'm experiencing in the church . . .

Cathedral Light

As you rest in the cathedral,
direct your attention to its darkness.

Now,
pay attention to the various ways in which light is present.

Both the darkness and light
are meant to enhance your prayers.

In the midst of the light and darkness in the church, I pray . . .

If You Are Looking for It

First impressions can be deceptive.
My first impression of the Chartres labyrinth
didn't even register beyond the moment.
The eight-hundred-year-old labyrinth is very understated
below the rows of wooden chairs that rest on its face.
It does peek out in the aisle,
but with so much else to look at in the cathedral, one seldom looks down.

When they do spot it, tourists are sometimes curious
about the pattern on the floor.
They usually look at the labyrinth quizzically for a moment, and then move on.

Pilgrims who come in search of the labyrinth always find it.
Not far inside the western door,
it covers the entire width of the main section of the church.
What you seek informs what you find.

I am seeking . . .

Where to Go

Pilgrimage sites can overwhelm
the senses and mind.
There is so much to see,
experience, learn, and understand.

Let these questions help orient you:
Where at this pilgrimage site can I love
God most deeply?
Where can I receive God's love most fully?

Knowing the answers will change over
time, respond now.
Go where Love is calling.

Love is inviting me to . . .

Correspondence

In Chartres Cathedral medieval catechumens are reported to have moved
from the baptismal font in the crypt up the stairs,
through the labyrinth pathway to its center,
and up the center of the nave to the altar.
This is where they received their first communion.

Connections that exist throughout the cathedral,
whether obvious or subtle, can be experienced
through the lenses of architecture, liturgy, theology, and history.

Connections that are becoming clearer to me as I spend time in the cathedral . . .

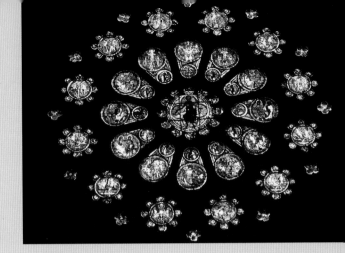

Beauty

In the cathedral,
one becomes particularly aware of the gentle but persistent power of beauty.
Beauty speaks.
Beauty resonates.
Beauty surrounds.
Beauty reminds.
Beauty calls.
Beauty disseminates its subtle but profound messages with countless voices.
Beauty travels far and wide in the bodies of those who have visited.

I'm encountering Beauty at Chartres in . . .

Paradoxical Space

Light and dark.
Empty and full.
Colossal and comfortable.
Ancient and modern.

From under one and the same roof
one can observe the meeting of so many opposites.

In Chartres Cathedral things hold together
in unexpected ways.

Paradoxes I'm observing . . .

F I V E

Deeper Explorations of the Cathedral

All year long tour buses arrive in Chartres. They transport those who come for a quick tour of the cathedral, light a few prayer candles, perhaps attend mass, and visit a gift shop or two before heading to the next destination.

A longer stay is required for those who want to know the cathedral more intimately. Some groups of pilgrims come to Chartres and remain for a few days or a week as they study, pray, and enjoy the town. Other pilgrims come by themselves and settle in. The value of an extended visit becomes more obvious the longer one stays.

Vision

With the benefit of hindsight,
pilgrims speak of traveling great distances
to discover
what was right in front of them
or what was already within them.

Right in front of me,
Right within me . . .

Why Am I Here?

It's a simple question: "Why am I here?"
If only the answer were simple to hear!
The answer may change from day to day.

As one keeps posing the question,
then listening with openness,
responses, engaging one another,
will point towards deeper understanding.

I am here to . . .

Each day, ask yourself again, "Why am I here?"

Meaning

To sit with the question
"What does it mean?"
while waiting for understanding
is not only worthwhile,
it can be transformative.

What meanings are being revealed?
Insight often follows attention.

Ask with an open mind.
Listen with an open heart.
Ask, "What does it mean?"

Meanings that are being revealed . . .

Activity and Noise

For some, the activity and noise in the cathedral
seem distracting.
For others,
they help bring focus to the experience of prayer.

I am discovering that when I am praying,
the activity and noise of the cathedral . . .

Inner and Outer Greetings

As you linger in this hallowed space,
notice how the Sacred
embodied in you
greets the Sacred
embodied in the cathedral.

Stay alert
and aware.

My embodied greetings . . .

Staying Present

When experiencing a sacred site for an extended time,
pilgrims may feel overstimulated.

If you begin to sense yourself becoming mentally or emotionally overloaded,
find a place to sit quietly.

Allow yourself to rest in this amazing context.
You can draw, journal, or simply be present to the moment in stillness.

When visiting the cathedral for longer periods of time, it helps me to . . .

Synchronicity

Many pilgrims mention
unexpected coincidences
that both surprise and delight them.

Things might work out better
than you planned!
Be open to the unexpected.
Enjoy the opportunity
to be out of control.

Synchronicities of my pilgrimage . . .

Distractions

Sometimes the work of pilgrimage seems too intense.
At this point a pilgrim can either choose to stay with the discomfort, and grow,
or use distractions as a way of avoiding what needs to experienced.

Activities like shopping,
having a lengthy cup of tea with an acquaintance,
or taking a nap
can support the pilgrim,
but not when used as a way of escaping sacred invitations.

The urge to distract oneself is normal.
If indulged, it can derail the momentum of the pilgrimage.

*Strategies I am finding helpful when the desire to distract myself
makes itself felt . . .*

Dreaming

It is not uncommon for dreams to support growth.

One night on pilgrimage I dreamt of a dear friend.
She was moving on the Chartres labyrinth.
Kate walked into a lightning bolt
whose purpose was her enlightenment.

Notes and images relating to a dream I've had on this pilgrimage . . .

Sacred Change

Spiritual openness is often cited by pilgrims
as one of their deepest desires.

When remaining open, it is not unusual for a pilgrim
to be invited by the Sacred to move into a new phase of relationship.

The death of one's previously valued experience of Divine Connection
can be very unsettling, even traumatic.
Being thrust into new rapport with the Holy is a challenge.

Be forewarned: openness often leads to change.
Change, even when it is the stated goal, requires courage.
Take heart! Grace supplies the needed nerve.

Spiritually disorienting experiences I'm weathering . . .

Companions

Relationships season
one's pilgrimage.
New acquaintances
are encountered daily.

Laughter,
shared meals,
prayer,
casual conversations,
sacred settings,
and profound questions
offer opportunities
for bonds of friendship
to be formed.

Whom am I meeting?

Whose companionship am I coming to value?

New Beginnings

How would you answer the question
"What has begun to develop within?"

Remember that this information
may not be available to your conscious mind.

Play with the ideas and images that emerge.
Try to enjoy not being sure yet.
Look harder for clues than for answers.

Developing within . . .

Lighting a Prayer Candle

Candles are available in the cathedral.
After making a donation,
pilgrims are welcome to light them as symbols of their prayers.
They can also be taken home.

Before lighting a candle, ask:
What sacred connection does this candle symbolize?
Why are fire and light helpful metaphors for prayer?
What words might best express the longed-for hope?
What gestures could embody my heart's deepest desires?

Questions have paved the way to this bit of wax and string.
Now it is time to pray.

Prayers that I would like to offer as I light this candle
as a symbol of my hopes, desires, and faith . . .

S I X

The Chartres Cathedral Labyrinth

Many who come to Chartres Cathedral are not aware of the labyrinth. They may see it and wonder, "What's this?" Others come with the express intention of experiencing the labyrinth that was laid into the floor around 1201 C.E. This circular pattern has a diameter of approximately forty-two feet and three inches. Most days, the majority of the pattern rests beneath rows of wooden chairs that fill the nave of the church. Its opening, bits of its pathway, and part of its center are exposed by the aisle created between the chairs.

The experience of praying the labyrinth in Chartres Cathedral is something pilgrims are likely to remember for the rest of their lives. In using this ancient spiritual tool, one walks on beautiful stone as pilgrims have done for centuries, giving one a sense of having entered holy history. As one moves on this circular pattern, different views of the cathedral's architecture and stained glass come and go, inspiring, comforting, challenging, reassuring. There is a pervading sense of safety within the magnificent sacred space of the dark cathedral. The sounds and sights of a parish at work and prayer add their flavor to the encounter as well.

This chapter introduces the pilgrim to the labyrinth within its context in the Chartres Cathedral and makes suggestions for using it.

Church Labyrinth

Labyrinths have been identified in many different settings.
This labyrinth, incorporated into the floor, is situated in a church.

Everything in a medieval cathedral was included
because of its potential for teaching spiritual truth.
However, there are no historical documents
that shed light on the designers' intentions for the Chartres labyrinth.
Documentation relating to medieval labyrinths
indicates that children enjoyed various games on labyrinths
and that clergy occasionally used church labyrinths for liturgical purposes.

Some suggest this labyrinth was thought of
and used as a symbolic road leading to salvation.
Others say it was used as a substitute pilgrimage
when it was too dangerous to visit the Holy Land.
There are those who claim it was used as a penitentiary tool
for seeking God's forgiveness.

We may desire to speculate about this labyrinth's original purposes,
or make educated guesses based on related historical documents,
but we can't say with certainty what this labyrinth was created to communicate
or the functions it served.

As I consider the Christian context of this cathedral labyrinth . . .

Placement

The Chartres labyrinth
has a six-petal center,
one hundred and thirteen
"teeth" around its perimeter,
and chalice-shaped path dividers.

It was built into the floor of the cathedral
where worshippers would gather.
Because it spans the entire width
of the nave,
the only way around it was to walk in one
of the side aisles.

It seems that those who envisioned
and built the labyrinth
wanted people to come in contact with it.

*After considering the placement
of the labyrinth, I . . .*

Teaching the Truths of Faith

Everything in a medieval cathedral was designed to teach the truths of the Christian way.

Proportion, geometry, shape, and theology were combined in service of faith.

Since most people were illiterate, symbols were used.

One significant teaching tool in Chartres Cathedral is the forty-two-foot circular labyrinth.

Cathedral symbols that are communicating truth to me . . .

The Chairs Covering the Labyrinth

It is hard for many pilgrims to understand
why the Chartres Cathedral labyrinth is usually covered with about 217 chairs.

Contemporary labyrinth use in the cathedral is relatively new.
While the cathedral staff has begun uncovering the labyrinth
one day a week during warmer weather,
they are still cautious about opening it at other times.
Change often occurs slowly, especially in cathedral settings.

While we wait for greater public access to the labyrinth,
let us pray with gratitude for those opportunities
to use the labyrinth that are made available.

My prayers for the labyrinth ministry of Chartres Cathedral . . .

Sitting Prayer

Sitting with the Chartres labyrinth can be prayer.
Sitting with it can also inspire prayer.

Explore the possibilities of sitting prayer
as you spend time near this sacred circle.
Once you get settled, sit quietly for at least twenty minutes.
Staying an hour would be more fruitful.

Sitting with the labyrinth, I am praying . . .

Roundness

The roundness of the labyrinth
would have immediately reminded medieval worshippers of other sacred realities
that they envisioned in a circular way:
the sun,
the cycles of nature,
the universe,
God.

The circular nature of the labyrinth calls forth . . .

Subtle Influences

If you look closely at the floor of Chartres Cathedral
you will notice that the labyrinth tilts gently towards the western wall.
Walking the labyrinth
involves moving up and down a subtle incline.

This gentle slope ensured that water used for cleaning the floor
would run towards the western doors
that could be opened to the outside.

While the slight angle of the floor eludes most visitors,
it is very obvious once one looks for it.

*Subtle influences that are shaping
my pilgrimage include . . .*

Cadence

Some speak of the rhythm of the Chartres labyrinth.

They note the symmetry of the pattern.
From outside to inside, and from side to side,
the path repeats itself.

One does not need to understand the blueprint of this beauty
to physically experience its message of balance.

While moving on the labyrinth's pathway, I perceive its rhythm in these ways . . .

Willem Kuipers discusses the cadence of the Chartres labyrinth pattern
in "Cadence Characterises Labyrinths" (*Caerdroia* 31:2000), pages 33–40.

Symbolism and Art

Robert Ferré, a leading authority on labyrinths,
was once asked,
"What do you make of the labyrinth in Chartres?"

He replied,
"It is a brilliant intellectual application of symbolism.
It is also an astounding work of art."

My understandings of the labyrinth as symbol and art . . .

Age Spots

The stones that comprise the labyrinth
are ancient,
and they show it!

Pockmarks,
worn areas,
holes,
and modern concrete "patches"
can all be spotted easily.

When I look carefully at the labyrinth, I notice . . .

Holy Ground

Many Americans like to walk the labyrinth without their shoes.
Some explain this desire by quoting Exodus 3:5:
"Remove the sandals from your feet,
for the place on which you are standing is holy ground."
Others suggest that people who are used to walking
and protecting canvas labyrinths get in the habit of leaving shoes behind.

Some pilgrims to Chartres are warned,
"Wear socks; the cathedral floor is very dirty!"
Even so, people can be seen taking off their shoes and socks
before entering the labyrinth.

Many Europeans find this odd at best, even offensive.
Cultural expectations about taking off shoes vary.
When seeing people walking without shoes onlookers sometimes wonder,
"Is this an esoteric practice used to connect with the energy of the ground?"
For some it is.
Making direct contact with a beloved spiritual tool appeals to different people
for different reasons.

When it comes to taking off my shoes to walk this labyrinth . . .

The View from the Threshold

Arriving, I peer down a long corridor,
yet see no destination at its end.
Glancing to my right and left, I notice colorful stories,
their glowing details inviting later exploration.
As I move my eyes to the horizon,
a monumental representation of glory arrests my vision.
As I look, incredible hues of blue open my heart.
Gazing down, I wonder at the miniature craters with their centuries-old history.
I open myself to the soaring majesty above,
the brilliant beauty behind,
and the calm surrounding darkness.
Desire calls me forward.

My poem about the labyrinth in Chartres . . .

What's Here

Begin moving on the
Chartres Cathedral labyrinth.

Wonder,
What is above this labyrinth?

Wonder,
What is below this labyrinth?

Wonder,
What is around this labyrinth?

My wonderings led me to . . .

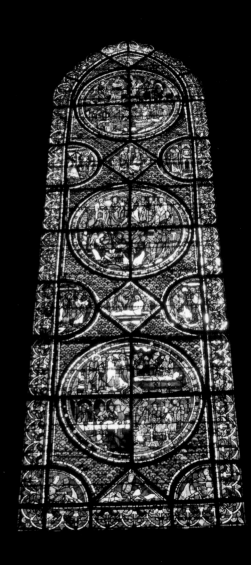

Turning Around

Pilgrimage often involves an honest assessment of life.
Confronted with the truth of the past and present,
pilgrims often feel a desire to change.

The concept of making a 180-degree turn
is embedded in the Greek word for repentance in the New Testament
and in the structure of the Chartres labyrinth.

Opportunities for practicing the art of changing
abound as one moves on the Chartres labyrinth.
There are twenty-eight u-turns on the way from the threshold to the center
and the same number as one moves from the center back to the threshold.

Experiment with embodying prayers of repentance
as you turn on the path.

Embodying repentance, I . . .

Stained Glass Windows

The stained glass windows that can be seen easily from the labyrinth include the west rose and the three large windows below it, which represent the life of Christ, his genealogy, and the history of his passion and resurrection.
The Mary window in the east and the tall windows flanking it
show the annunciation and visitation.
The Noah, St. Lubin, St. Eustache, and Joseph windows are to the north, and the St. John the Evangelist, Mary Magdalene, good Samaritan,
and death and assumption of Mary windows are to the south.

Choose one or more of the stories that is told in glass
to be the catalyst for your prayer on the labyrinth.

Prayers inspired by the stained glass windows around the labyrinth . . .

The Labyrinth as a Well

In the crypt of Chartres Cathedral
lies an ancient well.

The labyrinth has the same circular shape.
It too holds the possibility of refreshment.

As you move on the labyrinth,
imagine it as a well.

Draw up from its depths
what you need.

Having been to the well of the labyrinth . . .

Up Close and Personal

Read the following poem,
walk the labyrinth,
and then write a poem in response.

Labyrinth Reflections

Your beauty is my hope.
Your blemishes are my comfort.
Your vibration is my inspiration.
You potential is my calling.

My poem . . .

One Foot in Front of the Other

Between here and there
is one significant step.
Then another.
Then another.

What next step am I willing to take in my life?

What Does It Mean?

Once while walking the labyrinth in Chartres,
I overheard a young woman ask, "What does it mean?"

Her companion didn't answer, but kept walking
as if to say, "Your experience will help you understand."

If asked, "What does the labyrinth mean?" I would respond . . .

SEVEN

Pilgrims' Prayers

Pilgrims' prayers take a multitude of forms. The content of these prayers is as varied as the complexities of life. Often prayers are short, a word or two expressing the desire of an entire heart. Other prayers, wordless, can be observed, a slight or dramatic action embodying deeply felt needs and desires. Questions addressed to the Sacred, wonderings that spring from the hope of faith, often find their way into the hearts and minds of pilgrims. Short thoughts sometimes lead to long conversations with God.

Pilgrims pray in whatever ways are most meaningful, connecting with the Holy about everything. Included in this chapter are brief prayers intended to serve as springboards for your pilgrimage prayers.

How Long?

How long does it take
to make a meaningful connection
with the Sacred?
Two seconds? Thirty minutes?
Less than a moment?
Longer than a lifetime?
It can always happen now.

When I connect with the Sacred . . .

I'm Here

God,
I've come.
I'm here.

What now?

My prayers of uncertainty . . .

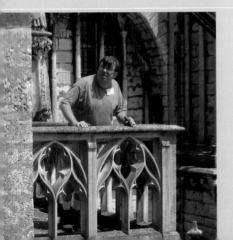

Openings

May my heart
and mind
become more open.

My prayers for openness . . .

Ears to Hear

Sacred Sound,
May I not only listen,
May I also hear.

My prayer for receptivity . . .

Widening Gratitude

On the way,
God,
may the gratitude
that rises from the
spring of Love
flow ever more strongly,
and thus widely.
May it be more so.

*My prayer for a
fuller experience
of gratitude ...*

Inner Awareness

May my inner landscape
become more available.

My prayer for deeper experiences of my inner self . . .

Growing Trust

I trust that all will be well,
but I wonder,
will it really?

May I trust more,
and wonder less.

My prayer for growing trust . . .

Love

May I be loved.
May I be love.

My love prayer . . .

When It Is Time

May these overwhelming birth pains do their job—
may I release what is ready to emerge.

My prayer for new life . . .

Depletion and Renewal

My reserves are running low,
exhaustion, discouragement, and confusion
are at an all-time high.

Sacred Rest,
can we pause for a while?

My prayer for renewal . . .

Write a Prayer

Write a prayer.
Write the words
that are already written in your heart.

If you must, write a draft;
don't fear its rough form.

Write
until you cannot write.
Which is to say
pray
until you need not pray.

Then stop.

The prayer that is already written in my heart . . .

Center of All

From Your center, from my center,
I wonder, "Where are You?"
You are here.
You are also at the headwaters
of this question's journey.
From here, and there
You extend in every direction, every dimension.
You are here,
but You are also not here.
No one place could ever limit You.

My prayer to the Center of All . . .

Grounding

May I trust the earth below my feet
to support me.

May I trust the Holy beyond and within me
to hold me securely.

My prayer for trust . . .

Drawing Close

I am here,
held,
and safe.

I will not squirm off Your lap.
Instead I will lean into Your strength,
feel Your warmth, and
let my heartbeat be synchronized
with Yours.

I am grateful.

The prayer my body knows to pray . . .

Waking Up

In the morning, as my body wakes,
I pray for my spirit to rouse itself as well.

Awakening, I pray . . .

Morning Devotions

Be waiting at the door to the cathedral
when it is unlocked.
The church is relatively quiet early in the morning
before tourists and tour groups begin arriving.
Immediately make your way to the labyrinth.
Find a place on the labyrinth to sit and pray.
It will likely be covered with chairs: use one!
Quiet yourself.
Notice any gratitude that you are experiencing
and allow it to expand.
Follow the devotional routine you use at home.
Pray. Meditate. Write. Draw. Breathe. Read. Contemplate.
Allow the energy of the labyrinth to support you.

After quieting myself . . .

Remembering Others Along the Way

Sometimes pilgrims travel by themselves,
but they do not stop caring about those left at home.

As loved ones come to mind and heart,
prayers are offered.

In Chartres Cathedral,
many prayer candles testify to this.

My prayers for those far away . . .

Local Devotional Practices

Those visiting pilgrimage sites have often discovered how valuable it can be to participate in the local devotional practices.

In Chartres Cathedral
it is not difficult to spot someone praying with a rosary.
Groups do this too, especially in the afternoons
at the regularly scheduled rosary service
held in the chapel that surrounds Notre Dame du Pilier.

The prayer beads of a rosary
can be used with traditional prayers,
or in any other way that one imagines might be useful.

While praying with a rosary in Chartres Cathedral . . .

Looking through the Labyrinth

Find a comfortable place to sit
where you can see as much of the labyrinth as possible.

Imagine that the labyrinth is an icon
through which you can experience God's presence.
Express your sense of love, devotion, and appreciation for the Divine
using both your eyes and your heart.

Gaze softly at the labyrinth for at least ten more minutes.
Remain open.
Accept whatever comes.

I saw and experienced . . .

The Sancta Camisa

The cathedral relic is a first-century cloth
that is reported to have been worn by Mary
during the annunciation of her pregnancy or at Jesus' birth.
It was given to the cathedral by Charles the Bald in 876.

Go and sit near the reliquary that holds a piece of the cathedral relic.
Notice the prayers that you want to pray when you are there.

Then, if the labyrinth is uncovered, go there.
Before entering it, imagine draping the relic over your shoulders
or some other part of your body.

Wearing this imaginary cloth of immense significance,
move on the labyrinth as a prayer.

Wearing the Sancta Camisa, I prayed . . .

Sacred Songs

Pilgrimages often include experiences that challenge
one's beliefs, commitments, hopes,
and relationship with the Divine.

Sometimes it becomes hard to pray.

A pilgrim once noted,
"I can sing to God
what I cannot say to God."

God, I am offering this song to you . . .

Surrender

This prayer is appropriate for every situation encountered on pilgrimage, "Thy will be done."

My prayer of surrender . . .

Sharing

Togetherness,
separateness,
where does one end
and the other begin?

There is so much I don't know,
so much You haven't communicated.

If love is not Your center,
I am truly lost.

***The thoughts I want to share
with God in prayer . . .***

Courage, Please!

It's a two-word prayer
that expresses deep need.

Even though I don't have to,
I want to pray it again.

Courage,
please!

My prayer for courage

Brokenness

The woman's body hobbles painfully by.
Her spirit goes ahead unimpeded.
I keep moving
while I invite You to keep moving with her.

If being healed
means becoming more whole,
please heal me
and those around me.

*My prayer for healing for myself
and those around me right now . . .*

Supporting Other Pilgrims

May my prayers
water the soil of this pilgrimage site
so that the seeds of hope
that others plant here
grow and blossom.

May it be so!

*My prayer of support
for other pilgrims . . .*

Gratitude

God,
may the gratitude I feel
be the origin of much grace
for others.

Thank You.
Thank You.
Thank You.

My prayer of gratitude . . .

E I G H T

Questions to Ponder

The experience of pilgrimage raises all sorts of
questions that are not likely to be answered quickly or
easily. It is important to honor the questions that emerge
by being willing to live with them over time. Consider
the questions in this chapter and add your own.

The Inside View

How can such beauty
be so immense?

How can such enormity
feel so natural and nurturing?

Is this what it is like to be one cell,
then two,
inside our mother's womb?

Chartres Cathedral makes me wonder about . . .

The Bigger Picture

What needs are met by the current worldwide labyrinth revival?
What is the work of the labyrinth in the church?
In society?
Globally?

The labyrinth is needed . . .

Perspective

Sacred connections
shift perceptions.

What in my life needs to change?

Blooming Season

How can a flower bloom continuously
for over eight hundred years?

Gazing at the flower in the center of the Chartres labyrinth, I wonder . . .

Growing Responsiveness

Surprises abound during pilgrimage.
Some of the most significant surprises
of all can come
when one experiences the equivalent
of a sacred kick in the pants!
In retrospect, these occurrences
are often highlights of one's journey.
At the time, they usually seem like
potentially insurmountable crises.

When you consider your pilgrimage,
what moments and experiences
have almost overwhelmed you
with the need to grow?

Growing . . .

The Labyrinths Within

In Chartres Cathedral, the labyrinth is in plain view.
Yet one can only find it when one has gone inside the cathedral,
and only when one is not distracted by everything else there is to see.

If you were to journey within your own body,
what labyrinths,
both visible and invisible,
would you find?

Inside me . . .

Considering Circles

You have spent time in a cathedral filled
with circles of every size imaginable!

What circle,
physical or metaphorical,
are you being invited to create,
appreciate in a new way,
or care for?

I am willing to . . .

Accepting the Invitation

To which of the many divine invitations
being offered during your pilgrimage
are you still willing to say,
"Yes!"?

I say "Yes!" to . . .

Traveling Inside

When leaving on pilgrimage,
you traveled to Chartres.
Now the pilgrimage site
exists within you in your memory.
Once you return home,
can you imagine ways
to revisit Chartres Cathedral
and its labyrinth
without returning physically?

Revisiting Chartres . . .

Being a Pilgrim

What do you mean when you say,
"I am a pilgrim"?

Being a pilgrim means . . .

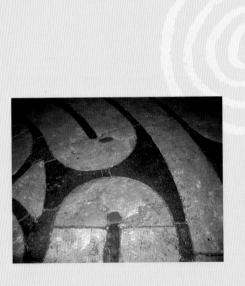

Part Four

R E T U R N I N G   H O M E

The time for returning home usually comes before the pilgrim feels ready! The thought of incorporating all that has been experienced and learned into the life that one left can seem overwhelming and impossible. A fear of losing a sense of spiritual connection is often reported.

The need to make this transition invites the pilgrim to begin shifting her or his attention outward. Now is the time to consider how to let the experiences of the pilgrimage continue to teach, shape, and direct. Now is the time to begin sharing the wisdom that has been gleaned.

NINE

Turning Toward Home

Good-byes are important. They acknowledge the meaning of what has happened. They offer opportunities for final connections. They allow for a broad range of emotions to be acknowledged and felt. Saying good-bye to the site of one's pilgrimage may be difficult, but it is highly recommended. Use the suggestions found in this chapter to help you become more ready to leave Chartres.

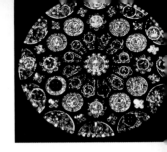

One More Thank-you

Return to a place where you have experienced the Holy
in a particularly meaningful way.

Before leaving, acknowledge the preciousness of your pilgrimage experiences
in that sacred space.

Find a way to express your gratitude.
Use a gesture, say a prayer,
or do anything else that comes to mind and heart.

In order to honor my experiences here,
I will go to . . .

and I will . . .

Don't Miss Your Opportunity

Transitions can be emotionally stressful. Some cope by leaving places and people without even saying good-bye.

Before I leave Chartres, I need to . . .

Appreciation and Grief

During transitions,
people often experience mixed emotions.

Take a few minutes to explore
any sense of gratefulness
that you are feeling.
Take several more minutes
to explore any sense of grief
that you are experiencing.
Honor both with your acceptance.

Embodying both gratefulness and grief . . .

Packing for the Return Trip

Before leaving for home,
take time to wonder with God,
"What words, images, feelings, and sounds
express the core of my pilgrimage experience?"

When you have identified them,
pack these gifts deep in your heart,
knowing that their remembrance will nourish you for years to come.

The gifts I'm taking home . . .

Thank-you Letter

Write a thank-you letter
to Jesus, or Mary, or God.

Express your gratitude
for specific gifts received during this pilgrimage.

Include favorite memories.
Share unanswered questions.
Mention those who touched your life.
Speak of your parting.

When the letter is finished, go to a favorite spot in the cathedral
and read the letter out loud or silently.

Dear . . .

Praying "Good-bye"

Before leaving the cathedral,
light one more candle
as you pray your hopes
for integrating this pilgrimage
experience into your life at home.

As I light this candle, I pray . . .

Pilgrim's Parting Prayer

Holy One,
Thank you! What a pilgrimage!

I cherish my memories of moments of laughter,
moments of passion,
moments of weeping, moments of creativity.

There has also been intense frustration,
deep joy, longing, questioning,
imagining, wondering.

It is time to move on.
My spirit resists even while accepting
the inevitable physical parting.

Thank You for the opportunities offered,
the connections shared,
and for the future birth of mysteries conceived.
Amen.

Holy One . . .

TEN

Telling the Story

Upon arriving home, a pilgrim is sure to be asked, "How was your trip?" There is so much to tell, how can one decide where to start? Most people are asking more out of courtesy than true interest. Considering how you want to respond is time well spent. Use the exercises in this chapter to help.

Let Me Show You

Use this page for creating a visual aid that you can use to share the meanings of your pilgrimage with others.

Names of three people to whom I will show this:

1.

2.

3.

Continuing to Share Your Story

Although the desire is there,
it often feels impossible to express
to others the importance
and meanings of one's pilgrimage experiences.

The more you integrate what you have experienced
into the life you live at home,
the greater will be your understanding and your ability to express it.

As time passes,
revisit your pilgrimage experiences with those who will listen carefully.
In the meantime,
come up with a one- to two-sentence reply to the question, "How was your trip?"

When people ask about my pilgrimage, I want to say . . .

PILGRIMS' PATHS
TO AND FROM CHARTRES

Nothing
and no one
is what we imagine at first.

More complicated, less one-dimensional,
we emerge from praying resurrected,
although we didn't realize we were dead.

Kilometers come and go,
opportunities are seized and missed,
we connect, we separate,
are filled, become empty—over and over.

Quiet and silence invite our presence,
sacred patterns invite our exploration,
metaphors, embodied in us, invite our honesty.

Searching, seeking, we reach out
to the waiting embrace of
Challenge, Hope, and Transformation.
Harmony rises before our bodies,
then resonates within us,
our memory hears it, feels it, sees it, recalls it fully.

Through the passageway of the heart
we are arriving home,
only to realize we need to keep moving.

L IST OF I MAGES

Except as otherwise noted, all images were taken by the author, © Jill Kimberly Hartwell Geoffrion, at the Chartres Cathedral.

DEDICATION

Cheryl Felicia Dudley sitting on one of the pillar "benches"; Tim Geoffrion on one of the upper walkways of the cathedral; Monsieur Christian Gaudinière in the cathedral; Madame Patricia Devriendt arranging flowers, welcome desk; Monsieur Dartus Yves singing on south porch steps; Robert Ferré, south porch steps

PART ONE ▪ PREPARATION FOR PILGRIMAGE

1, Lisa Gidlow Moriarty, Dancing Lady Labyrinth, Minnesota

Chapter One ▪ Readying Yourself

3, Ruth Hanna, Secret Garden Labyrinth, Minnesota; 5, Cheryl Felicia Dudley, the Charism Labyrinth; 6, Lisa Gidlow Moriarty mowing a grass labyrinth, Minneapolis, Minnesota; 7, Seaweed Labyrinth, Copamarina, Puerto Rico © Daniel Eugene Geoffrion; 8, Shadow of labyrinth walker, Minnesota; 9, Camp Coldwater Labyrinth, Minnesota; 10, French sign of gratitude © Cheryl Felicia Dudley; 11, Deep Haven prayer group; 12, Pam Kearney, Camp Courage temporary labyrinth; 13, Suitcase; 14, Friends and family, three-circuit labyrinth, Minnesota; 15, French church pillars © Timothy Charles Geoffrion

List of Images

List of Images

light on stained glass windows, Chartres Cathedral; 110, Door from south porch into the cathedral; 111, Prayer candles, south transept, Chartres; 112, Notre Dame du Pilier and Jesus © Cheryl Felicia Dudley; 113, The Chartres labyrinth; 114, Carving of the Sancta Camisa that is found throughout the cathedral; 115, Column figure, west wall; 116, Steps to the St. Piat chapel; 117, West windows: the rose and three lower stained glass windows; 118, Flying buttresses; 119, Labyrinth turns; 120, Gardens of the Beaux Arts Museum next to the cathedral; 121, South rose window and lancets © Cheryl Felicia Dudley

Chapter Eight ▪ Questions to Ponder

122, Creatures under column figure, west wall; 123, Inside the cathedral in the morning before the "daytime lights" have been turned on; 124, Turns, labyrinth; 125, Aisle supports, north side of the cathedral; 126, Center, labyrinth; 127, Lion, north tower; 128, Meeting point, labyrinth; 129, Window under restoration, south ambulatory; 130, St. Piat chapel tower; 131, North tower; 132, Labyrinth turns

PART FOUR ▪ RETURNING HOME

133, Pilgrimage marker, Chartres

Chapter Nine ▪ Turning Towards Home

135, Author on the way to the train station in Chartres; 136, South rose window; 137, The Angel of the Sundial, south side of cathedral; 138, View of Chartres from the north tower; 139, Stained glass panel, Chartres; 140, Stained glass window of Mary offering her breast to Jesus, above Notre Dame de Belle Verrière, south apse © Cheryl Felicia Dudley; 142, Prayer candles, north ambulatory; 143, Christ in judgment, west wall

Chapter Ten ▪ Telling the Story

144, The west wall, Chartres Cathedral; 146, Shell, small choir sculpture

Information about Labyrinth Availability

156, Girl looking at the labyrinth

R e s o u r c e s / B i b l i o g r a p h y

Artress, Lauren. *Walking a Sacred Path: Rediscovering the Labyrinth as a Spiritual Tool.* New York: Riverhead Books, 1995.

Barron, Robert. *Heaven in Stone and Glass: Experiencing the Spirituality of the Great Cathedrals.* New York: Crossroad, 2000.

Cannota, Judy. "The Labyrinth: Praying Psalm 139." *Weavings* XVII, no. 3 (2003).

Clift, Jean Dalby, and Wallace B. Clift. *The Archetype of Pilgrimage: Outer Action with Inner Meaning.* Mahwah, N.J.: Paulist Press, 1996.

Coffey, Kathy. "Labyrinth Prayer." *Praying* 64 (Jan.–Feb. 1995): 20.

Cousineau, Phil. *The Art of Pilgrimage: The Seeker's Guide to Making Travel Sacred.* Berkeley, Calif.: Conari Press, 1998.

Doob, Penelope Reed. *The Idea of the Labyrinth from Classical Antiquity through the Middle Ages.* Ithaca, NY: Cornell University Press, 1990.

Favier, Jean. *The World of Chartres.* New York: Harry N. Abrams, 1988.

Ferré, Robert. *Origin, Symbolism, and Design of the Chartres Labyrinth.* St. Louis: One Way Press, 2001.

Geoffrion, Jill Kimberly Hartwell. *Praying the Labyrinth: A Journal for Spiritual Creativity.* Cleveland: Pilgrim Press, 1999.

_____ . *Labyrinth and the Song of Songs.* Cleveland: Pilgrim Press, 2003.

_____ . *Christian Prayer and Labyrinths: Pathways to Faith, Hope, and Love.* Cleveland, Pilgrim Press, 2004.

_____ . *Living the Labyrinth: 101 Paths to a Deeper Connection with the Sacred.* Cleveland: Pilgrim Press, 2004.

Resources/Bibliography

Chartres Cathedral: A Sacred Geometry. DVD, Janson Media, 2003.

James, John. "The Mystery of the Great Labyrinth: Chartres Cathedral." *Studies in Comparative Religion* 11 (1977): 92–115.

_____ . *The Master Masons of Chartres.* New York: West Grinstead Publishing, 1982.

Jones, Tony. "The Labyrinth." T*he Sacred Way: Spiritual Practices for Everyday Life.* Grand Rapids: Zondervan, 2004, 126-133.

Kern, Hermann. *Through the Labyrinth. Designs and Meanings over 5,000 Years.* New York: Prestel, 2000.

Legaux, Francois, and Marie-Josephe Deboos. *Chartres: Un Prêtre Raconte la Cathédrale.* Chartres, France: Éditions Houvet, 2002.

Miller, Malcolm. *Chartres Cathedral. Medieval Masterpieces in Stained Glass and Sculpture.* Andover, Hampshire, Great Britain: Pitkin Unichrome, 1994.

O'Roark, Mary Ann. "A Walk Through Time." *Guideposts* 54, no. 7 (September 1999): 40–43.

Prache, Anne. *Chartres Cathedral. Image of the Heavenly Jerusalem.* Paris: CNRS Editions, 1993.

Sands, Helen Raphael. *The Healing Labyrinth. Finding Your Path to Inner Peace.* New York: Barrons, 2001

Saward, Jeff, and Kimberly Lowelle Saward. "Is That a Fact?" *Caerdroia* 33 (2003): 14–27.

Strachan, Gordon. *Chartres: Sacred Geometry, Sacred Space.* Edinburgh: Floris Books, 2003.

Villette, Jean. *The Enigma of the Labyrinth.* St. Louis: One Way Press, 1995.

Wright, Craig. *The Maze and the Warrior. Symbols in Architechture, Theology, and Music.* Cambridge, Mass.: Harvard University Press, 2001.

INFORMATION ABOUT LABYRINTH AVAILABILITY

Contact the cathedral staff, in French, before you go to inquire about any specific dates when the labyrinth will be uncovered.

Service "Accueil-Visites" Cathédrale de Chartres
24, Cloitre Notre Dâme B.P. 131
28003 Chartres Cedex, France
From the United States: phone 011-33-2-37-21-75-02; fax 011-33-2-37-36-51-43
Email: visitecathedrale@diocesechartres.com
Website: www.diocesechartres.com/cathedrale

The schedule changes from year to year but in the recent past the labyrinth has been open most Fridays starting in Lent (March or April) through All Saints' Day (October). The labyrinth is not open during certain pilgrimage times in May, or during certain cathedral events that are scheduled at the last moment, such as funerals.

For the fewest distractions from tour groups and others that wander across the labyrinth unaware of its significance, plan to arrive when the cathedral opens or walk in the late afternoon.

In the past the cathedral has scheduled two guided labyrinth experiences a year. These are conducted in French. You may inquire at the welcome office about these.

It is possible to inquire about arranging labyrinth use for groups after hours by calling the French-speaking cathedral staff at 011-33-2-37-21-58-08 (from the United States). A form needs to be filled out and a donation is requested. You may also inquire about receiving the necessary form by email.